Calligraphy Practice Workbook

____

____

© 2024 Quillscribe Memoirs

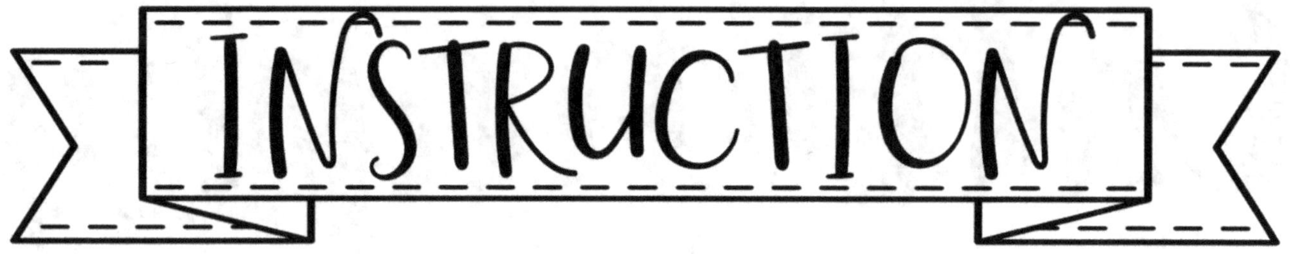

Fundamentals of Lettering

Mastering the art of lettering starts with a few basics. Good posture and pen grip may seem simple but are crucial for your progress.

Sitting Right

Consider your posture as the foundation of lettering. Sit where your feet are firmly on the ground, and you have enough space to move your arm freely. This position allows for better control. Use your other hand to keep the paper still for more precision.

Pen Mastery

When you grip your pen, aim for a balance – not too tight, not too loose. The angle of your pen is key to producing beautiful strokes. Don't worry if it's not perfect at first. Think of it as learning to walk; it takes time and persistence. Keep practicing, and you'll see your skills grow.

Essential Lettering Tools

If you're excited about starting lettering, you might want to buy all sorts of tools, but you really don't have to spend a lot. For our purposes, we'll stick to the basics: a Fudenosuke Pen and a Brush Pen. But here are some other tools you might consider:

Pencils: They're easy to find and good for beginners.

Pens: Start with any pen you have. Micron pens are nice, but even a gel pen or felt tip works.

Brush Pens: They're like fancy quill pens but be careful, they can be addictive and tricky to use at first.

Watercolors: Fun for creating with colors, you can use different brushes for different effects.

Chalk: You can find special markers to create chalk designs that look stunning.

Paper: The book has space for practice, but for more practice, get some thick card stock paper. It's better than regular thin paper.

Fudenosuke Pen: We're using this fine-tipped pen in the book for neat, single-line writing. You can buy it at any craft store.

Brush Pen: Great for when you want to try more elaborate calligraphy and designs.

Learning Strokes

This style is sometimes called "easy calligraphy" because it's straightforward and quick. It's all about making lines look even and smooth – like drawing with one of those cool pens you see on craft sites. You move your pen just like in the Brush Alphabet, but keep the pressure the same all the time. No need for heavy lines here! You can even use normal pens, but a smaller tip is better.

1 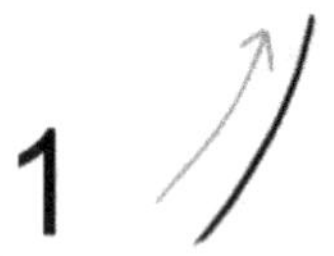 2 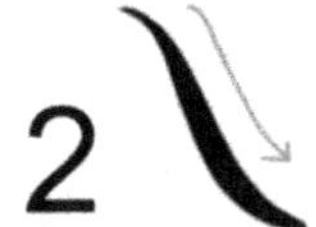 3 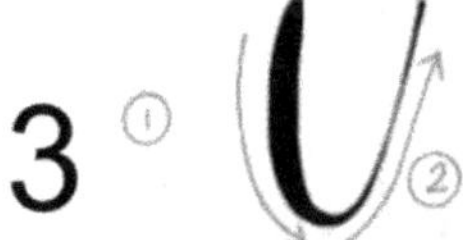 4 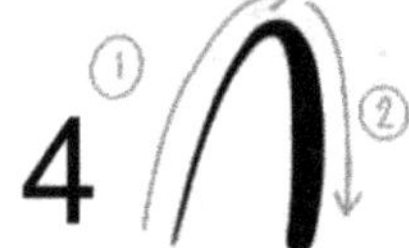

5 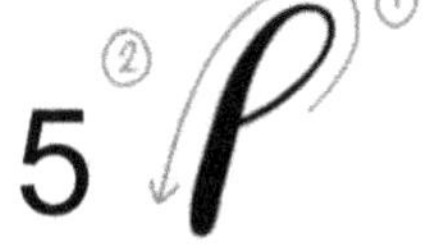 6 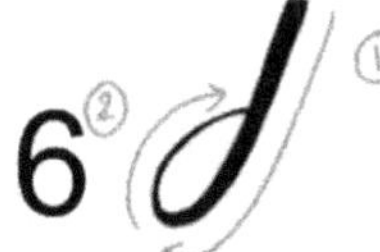 7 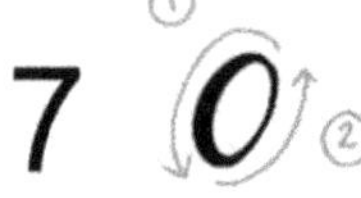 8 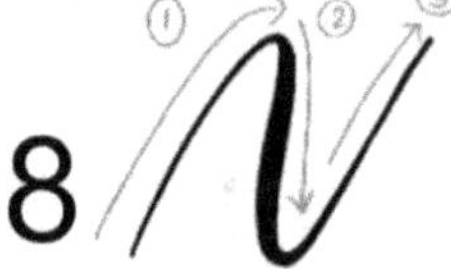

Strokes:

1 Light lines going up.

2 Heavy lines going down.

3 Curves starting from the bottom going up.

4 Curves starting from the top going down.

5 Loops reaching high.

6 Loops going low.

7 Shapes like an egg.

8 Fancy S-like shapes.

Upstrokes

Start from the bottom and go up.

Keep the line thin.

Don't press too hard.

Downstrokes

Start from the top and go down.

Press harder for a thicker line.

Start with less pressure, press more as you go down,
then let up at the end.

Underturn Stroke

Start with a thick line going down.

Then make a thin line going up.

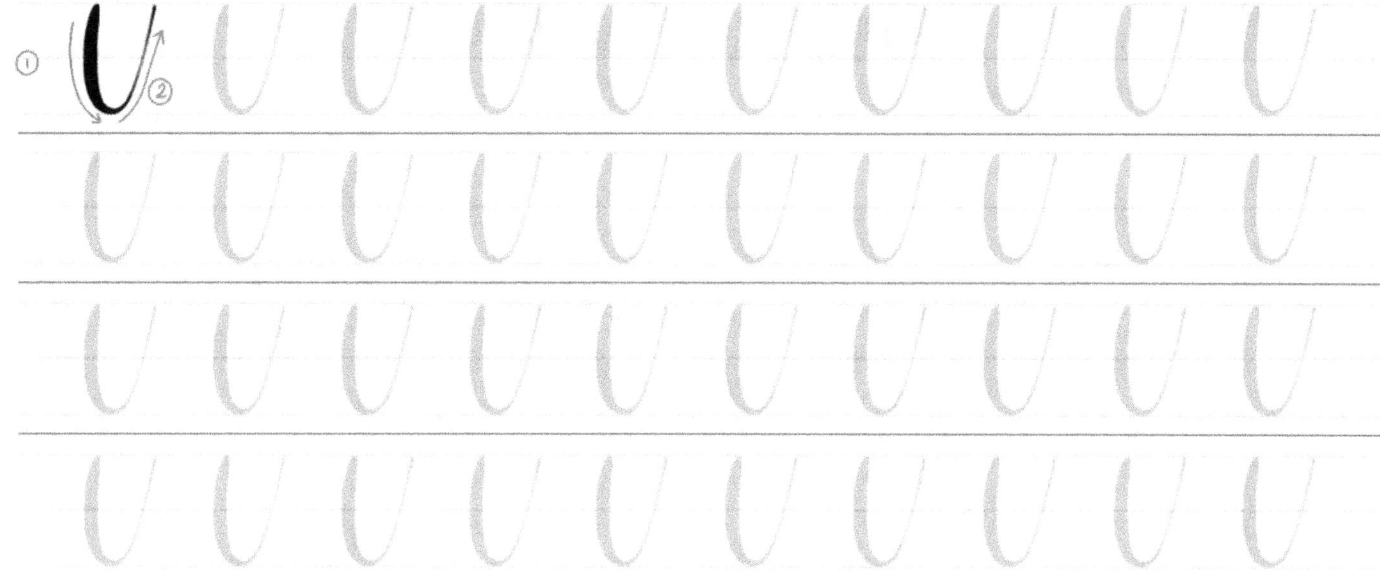

Overturn Stroke

Start with a thin line going up.

Then make a thick line going down.

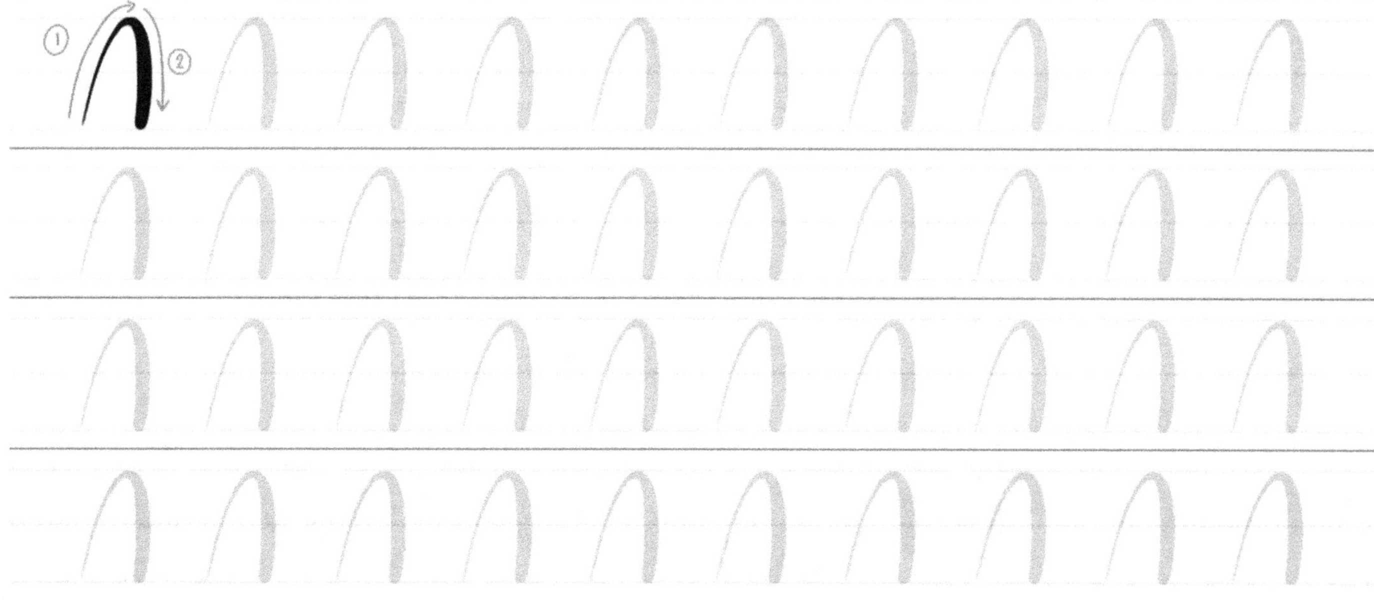

Ascending Loop

Make a thin line that curves up and over.

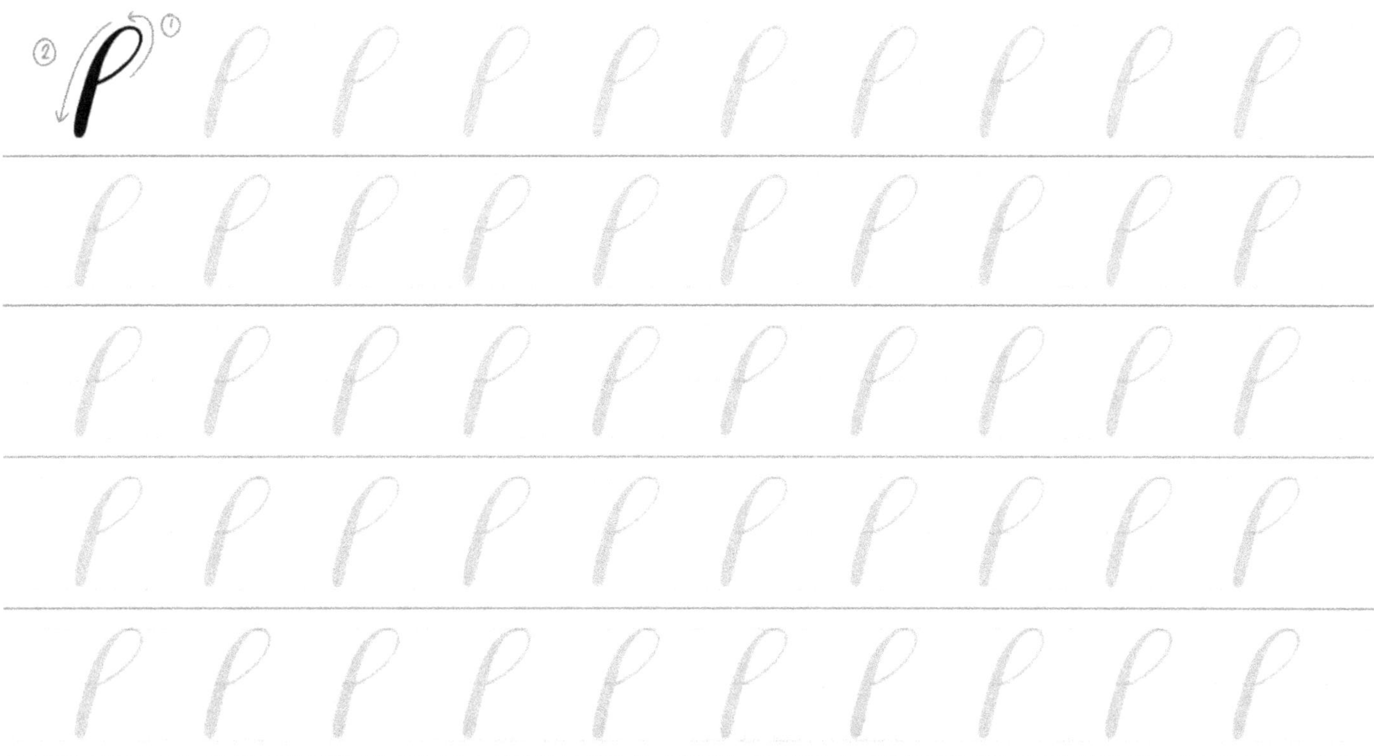

Descending Loop

Make a thin line that curves down and under.

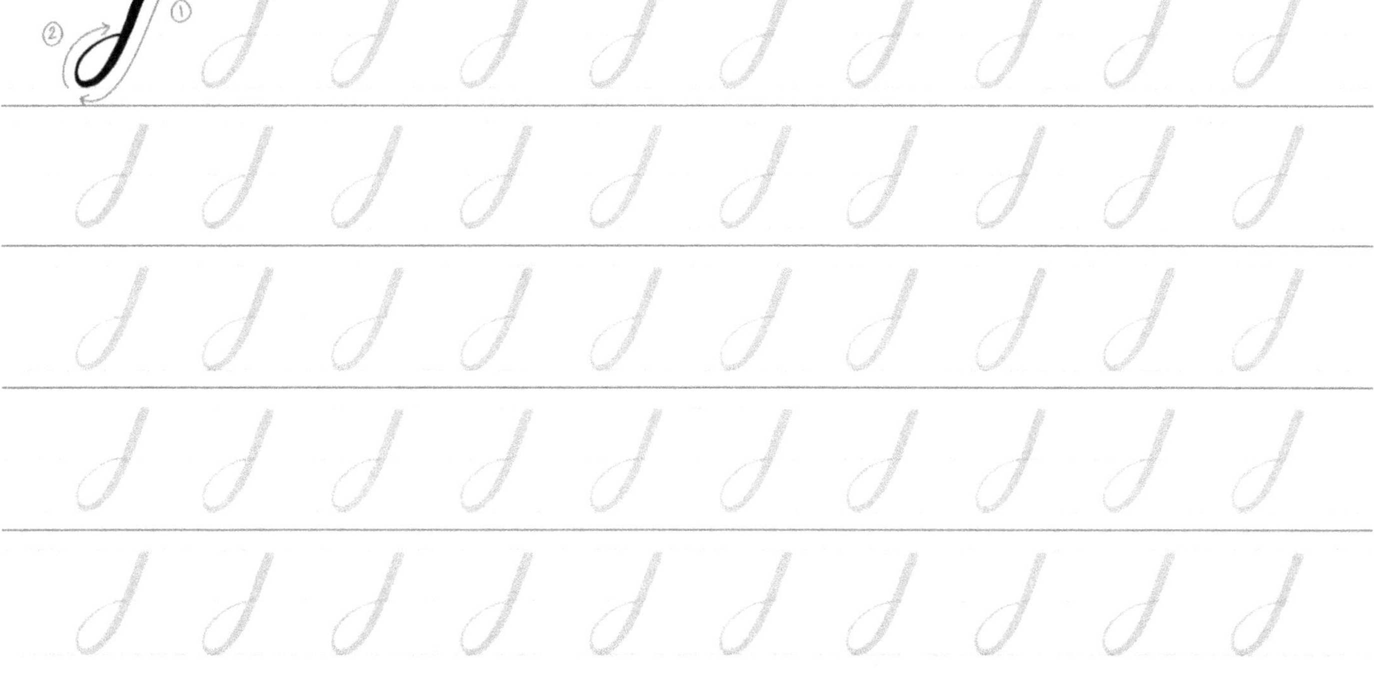

Oval

Make a looped shape like a sideways egg.

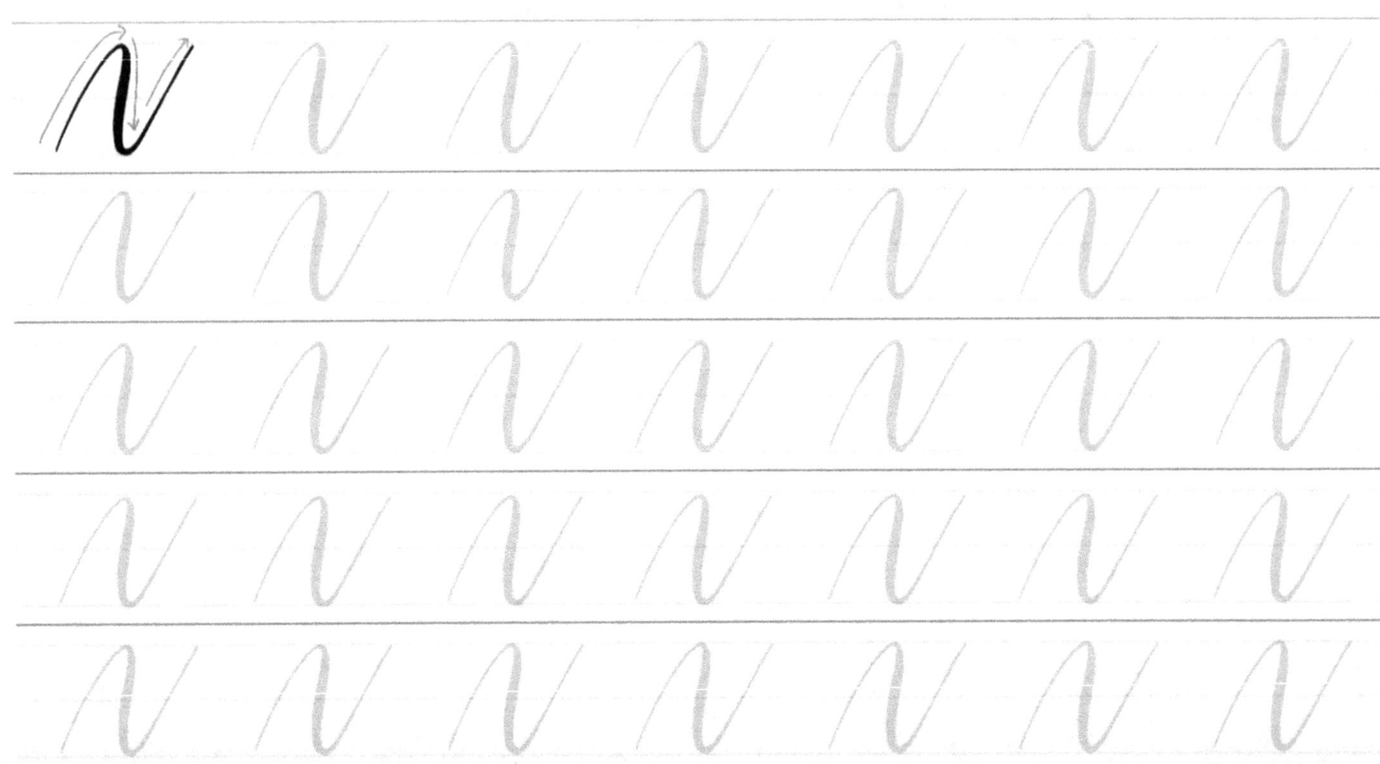

Compound Curve

Start with a curve up then a bigger curve down, like a wave.

Your practice unfolds in a tranquil garden where skills flourish, each in their own time. It's not solely the pursuit of flawless script that defines this journey, but the joy and serenity experienced with each stroke. Cherish every small triumph: the loop that forms perfectly, the flowing harmony of strokes uniting.

You wield not just a pen, but a wand that casts words into visual poetry. Your paper serves as a canvas, each word a reflection of your spirit. Treat yourself with kindness, allowing the positivity within to steer your hand. The true splendor of this voyage is in each moment spent, not merely the outcome.

Greet each new page with a smile, embracing the progress each represents. Every instance is a step forward, a cause for pride. Inhale deeply, releasing your creative spirit. The calligraphy world shines a little brighter with your presence.

Embrace this message, letting it nourish your practice sessions.

Happy writing!

LETTERS FOR SMALL BRUSH PENS

RECOMMENDED PEN: TOMBOW FUDE OR PENTEL SIGN PEN

Don't forget! Heavy Pressure on Your Downstroke & Light Pressure on Your Upstroke!

A A A A A A A A A A A A

A

A

a a a a a a a a a a a a

a

a

Ambition Ambition Ambition

Ambition Ambition Ambition

Ambition

LETTERS FOR SMALL BRUSH PENS

RECOMMENDED PEN: TOMBOW FUDE OR PENTEL SIGN PEN

Don't forget! Heavy Pressure on Your Downstroke & Light Pressure on Your Upstroke!

B

B

B

b

b

b

Brave

Brave

Brave

LETTERS FOR SMALL BRUSH PENS

RECOMMENDED PEN: TOMBOW FUDE OR PENTEL SIGN PEN

Don't forget! Heavy Pressure on Your Downstroke & Light Pressure on Your Upstroke!

C C C C C C C C C C C C

C

C

c c c c c c c c c c c c c

c

c

Courage Courage Courage

Courage

Courage

LETTERS FOR SMALL BRUSH PENS

RECOMMENDED PEN: TOMBOW FUDE OR PENTEL SIGN PEN

Don't forget! Heavy Pressure on Your Downstroke & Light Pressure on Your Upstroke!

b b b b b b b b b b

b

b

d d d d d d d d d d

d

d

Determination Determination Determination

Determination

Determination

LETTERS FOR SMALL BRUSH PENS

RECOMMENDED PEN: TOMBOW FUDE OR PENTEL SIGN PEN

Don't forget! Heavy Pressure on Your Downstroke & Light Pressure on Your Upstroke!

E E E E E E E E E E E E E E E E E

E

E

e e e e e e e e e e e e e e e e

e

e

Empowerment Empowerment

Empowerment Empowerment

Empowerment

LETTERS FOR SMALL BRUSH PENS

RECOMMENDED PEN: TOMBOW FUDE OR PENTEL SIGN PEN

Don't forget! Heavy Pressure on Your Downstroke & Light Pressure on Your Upstroke!

f f f f f f f f f f f f f f f

f

f

f f f f f f f f f f f f f f f

f

f

fortitude fortitude fortitude

fortitude

fortitude

LETTERS FOR SMALL BRUSH PENS

RECOMMENDED PEN: TOMBOW FUDE OR PENTEL SIGN PEN

Don't forget! Heavy Pressure on Your Downstroke & Light Pressure on Your Upstroke!

G G G G G G G G G G G

G

G

g g g g g g g g g g g

g

g

Growth Growth Growth

Growth

Growth

LETTERS FOR SMALL BRUSH PENS

RECOMMENDED PEN: TOMBOW FUDE OR PENTEL SIGN PEN

Don't forget! Heavy Pressure on Your Downstroke & Light Pressure on Your Upstroke!

H

H

H

h

h

h

Hope

Hope

Hope

LETTERS FOR SMALL BRUSH PENS

RECOMMENDED PEN: TOMBOW FUDE OR PENTEL SIGN PEN

Don't forget! Heavy Pressure on Your Downstroke & Light Pressure on Your Upstroke!

l

l

l

i

i

i

Inspiration

Inspiration

Inspiration

LETTERS FOR SMALL BRUSH PENS

RECOMMENDED PEN: TOMBOW FUDE OR PENTEL SIGN PEN

Don't forget! Heavy Pressure on Your Downstroke & Light Pressure on Your Upstroke!

J J J J J J J J J J J J J J J J

J

J

j j j j j j j j j j j j j j j j

j

j

Joy Joy Joy Joy

Joy

Joy

LETTERS FOR SMALL BRUSH PENS

RECOMMENDED PEN: TOMBOW FUDE OR PENTEL SIGN PEN

Don't forget! Heavy Pressure on Your Downstroke & Light Pressure on Your Upstroke!

K K K K K K K K K K K

K

K

k k k k k k k k k k k

k

k

Kindness Kindness Kindness

Kindness

Kindness

LETTERS FOR SMALL BRUSH PENS

RECOMMENDED PEN: TOMBOW FUDE OR PENTEL SIGN PEN

Don't forget! Heavy Pressure on Your Downstroke & Light Pressure on Your Upstroke!

L

L

L

l

l

l

Love

Love

Love

LETTERS FOR SMALL BRUSH PENS

RECOMMENDED PEN: TOMBOW FUDE OR PENTEL SIGN PEN

Don't forget! Heavy Pressure on Your Downstroke & Light Pressure on Your Upstroke!

M

M

M

m

m

m

Motivation

Motivation

Motivation

LETTERS FOR SMALL BRUSH PENS

RECOMMENDED PEN: TOMBOW FUDE OR PENTEL SIGN PEN

Don't forget! Heavy Pressure on Your Downstroke & Light Pressure on Your Upstroke!

n n n n n n n n n n n

n

n

n n n n n n n n n n n n n n

n

n

Nobility Nobility Nobility

Nobility

Nobility

LETTERS FOR SMALL BRUSH PENS

RECOMMENDED PEN: TOMBOW FUDE OR PENTEL SIGN PEN

Don't forget! Heavy Pressure on Your Downstroke & Light Pressure on Your Upstroke!

O

O

O

o

o

o

Optimism

Optimism

Optimism

LETTERS FOR SMALL BRUSH PENS

RECOMMENDED PEN: TOMBOW FUDE OR PENTEL SIGN PEN

Don't forget! Heavy Pressure on Your Downstroke & Light Pressure on Your Upstroke!

p

p

p

p

p

p

Passion

Passion

Passion

LETTERS FOR SMALL BRUSH PENS

RECOMMENDED PEN: TOMBOW FUDE OR PENTEL SIGN PEN

Don't forget! Heavy Pressure on Your Downstroke & Light Pressure on Your Upstroke!

Q Q Q Q Q Q Q Q Q

Q

Q

q q q q q q q q q

q

q

Quest Quest Quest

Quest Quest Quest

Quest

LETTERS FOR SMALL BRUSH PENS

RECOMMENDED PEN: TOMBOW FUDE OR PENTEL SIGN PEN

Don't forget! Heavy Pressure on Your Downstroke & Light Pressure on Your Upstroke!

R R R R R R R R R R R R

R

R

r r r r r r r r r r r r

r

r

Respect Respect Respect

Respect

Respect

LETTERS FOR SMALL BRUSH PENS

RECOMMENDED PEN: TOMBOW FUDE OR PENTEL SIGN PEN

Don't forget! Heavy Pressure on Your Downstroke & Light Pressure on Your Upstroke!

S S S S S S S S S S

S

S

s s s s s s s s s s s

s

s

Success Success Success

Success Success Success

Success

LETTERS FOR SMALL BRUSH PENS

RECOMMENDED PEN: TOMBOW FUDE OR PENTEL SIGN PEN

Don't forget! Heavy Pressure on Your Downstroke & Light Pressure on Your Upstroke!

T

T

T

t

t

t

Trust

Trust

Trust

LETTERS FOR SMALL BRUSH PENS

RECOMMENDED PEN: TOMBOW FUDE OR PENTEL SIGN PEN

Don't forget! Heavy Pressure on Your Downstroke & Light Pressure on Your Upstroke!

U U U U U U U U U U U

U

U

u u u u u u u u u u u

u

u

Unleash Unleash Unleash

Unleash Unleash Unleash

Unleash

LETTERS FOR SMALL BRUSH PENS
RECOMMENDED PEN: TOMBOW FUDE OR PENTEL SIGN PEN
Don't forget! Heavy Pressure on Your Downstroke & Light Pressure on Your Upstroke!

V
V
V
v
v
v
Victory
Victory
Victory

LETTERS FOR SMALL BRUSH PENS

RECOMMENDED PEN: TOMBOW FUDE OR PENTEL SIGN PEN

Don't forget! Heavy Pressure on Your Downstroke & Light Pressure on Your Upstroke!

W W W W W W W

W W W W W W W

W

w w w w w w w w

w w w w w w w w

w

Win Win Win Win

Win Win Win Win

Win

LETTERS FOR SMALL BRUSH PENS

RECOMMENDED PEN: TOMBOW FUDE OR PENTEL SIGN PEN

Don't forget! Heavy Pressure on Your Downstroke & Light Pressure on Your Upstroke!

X X X X X X X X X X X

X

X

x x x x x x x x x x x

x x x x x x x x x

x

X-factor

X-factor

X-factor

LETTERS FOR SMALL BRUSH PENS

RECOMMENDED PEN: TOMBOW FUDE OR PENTEL SIGN PEN

Don't forget! Heavy Pressure on Your Downstroke & Light Pressure on Your Upstroke!

Y Y Y Y Y Y Y Y Y Y

Y Y Y Y Y Y Y Y Y Y

Y

y y y y y y y y y y

y y y y y y y y y y

y

Yearn Yearn Yearn

Yearn Yearn Yearn

Yearn

LETTERS FOR SMALL BRUSH PENS

RECOMMENDED PEN: TOMBOW FUDE OR PENTEL SIGN PEN

Don't forget! Heavy Pressure on Your Downstroke & Light Pressure on Your Upstroke!

Z Z Z Z Z Z Z Z Z Z

Z

Z

Z

Z

Z

Zeal Zeal Zeal Zeal

Zeal Zeal Zeal Zeal

Zeal

NUMBERS FOR SMALL BRUSH PENS

RECOMMENDED PEN: TOMBOW FUDE OR PENTEL SIGN PEN

Don't forget! Heavy Pressure on Your Downstroke & Light Pressure on Your Upstroke!

1 1 1 1 1 1 1 1 1 1

1

1

2 2 2 2 2 2 2 2 2 2

2 2 2 2 2 2 2 2

2

3 3 3 3 3 3 3 3

3 3 3 3 3 3 3 3

3

NUMBERS FOR SMALL BRUSH PENS

RECOMMENDED PEN: TOMBOW FUDE OR PENTEL SIGN PEN

Don't forget! Heavy Pressure on Your Downstroke & Light Pressure on Your Upstroke!

4   4   4   4   4   4   4   4

4

4

5   5   5   5   5   5   5   5

5

5

6   6   6   6   6   6   6   6

6

6

NUMBERS FOR SMALL BRUSH PENS

RECOMMENDED PEN: TOMBOW FUDE OR PENTEL SIGN PEN

Don't forget! Heavy Pressure on Your Downstroke & Light Pressure on Your Upstroke!

NUMBERS FOR SMALL BRUSH PENS

RECOMMENDED PEN: TOMBOW FUDE OR PENTEL SIGN PEN

Don't forget! Heavy Pressure on Your Downstroke & Light Pressure on Your Upstroke!

Positive and inspiring

Dream big, start small

Dream big, start small

Grow through what you go through

Grow through what you go through

Choose joy every day

Choose joy every day

Positive and inspiring

Be the positive change

Be the positive change

Choose joy every single day

Choose joy every single day

Live every day with intention

Live every day with intention

Positive and inspiring

Create your own sunshine

Spread kindness everywhere

Always believe in yourself

Positive and inspiring

Dreams demand hustle

Be fearless in pursuit

Tomorrow needs your best today

Positive and inspiring

Keep moving forward

Keep moving forward

Challenge limits, discover strengths

Challenge limits, discover strengths

Own your mornings, energize days

Own your mornings, energize days

Positive and inspiring

Every moment is a chance

Adventure awaits, go seek

Craft your masterpiece

Positive and inspiring

Let passion light your way

Let passion light your way

Paint your dreams daily

Paint your dreams daily

Challenges sweeten victories

Challenges sweeten victories

Positive and inspiring

Setbacks pave comebacks

Setbacks pave comebacks

Seek joy in every day

Seek joy in every day

Act with purpose and passion

Act with purpose and passion

Positive and inspiring

Coffee spills, laughter follows

Coffee spills, laughter follows

Life's a dance, you lead

Life's a dance, you lead

You're doing wonderfully well

You're doing wonderfully well

Positive and inspiring

Happiness suits you beautifully

Happiness suits you beautifully

Kindness looks amazing on you

Kindness looks amazing on you

Authenticity is your superpower

Authenticity is your superpower

Love

Calm

Forward

friend

Admire

Balance

Empathy

Celebrate

Blessed

Dream

Awesome

Excited

Let's get creative!

Kind

Life

Heart

Kiss

Good

Loyal

Joy

Inspire

Giving

Mellow Hope Justice

Mindful

Ideal

You're doing awesome

Rise

pretty

Truthful

Overcome Nice

Queen

Reason

Optimist

Succeed Noble

Quick

Real

Strong

Please

Just keep going

Zest

Yes   Unique

Voyage   Wise   Zappy

Visualize Xen   Ultimate

Xenial   Warm   Youth

Work hard Dream big

persevere

Thrive

Inspire

Innovate

Achieve

Discover

Empower

Transform

Overcome

Unstoppable

Limitless

Fearless

Ascend

Illuminate

Triumph

don't look back,
you aren't going
that way

do small things
with
great love

always be
kind

You never fail
until you stop
trying

when things change inside you, things change around you

Sometimes, what you're looking for, comes when you're not looking at all

feel it so you can heal it

Just because
it's taking time
doesn't mean
it's not happening

you will get
where
you need to be

All I can do
is all I can do,
and that is
enough

from failure
comes clarity

Don't wait for your life to be perfect to enjoy it

— if it never rained, nothing would grow

often, the best answer is just to listen

do your best
forget the rest

Be patient with
everyone
but especially
yourself

plant the seeds for a brighter tomorrow

there is so much to be thankful for

A beautiful life starts with a beautiful perspective

it's better to start small than not at all

thankful for
where I am,
excited for
where I'm going
their opinions
are not your
problem

Sometimes
you win
sometimes
you learn

one step
at a time

give yourself
time to rest

focus on
improving, not
impressing

There's no "right time," just time and what you do with it.

Don't spend this moment wishing for another

change is inevitable, growth is optional

if it's out of your hands, it deserves freedom from your mind, too

don't lose your kindness in the chaos

the best time
for a new
beginning
is
now
live life
joyfully

you don't
have to
be perfect
to be loved
— stop and —
smell the
flowers

make today
great

She who is
BRAVE
is free

Your practice

Your practice

Your practice

Your practice

Your practice

Your practice

Your practice

As your pen lifts from the paper, take a moment to acknowledge the progress you've made today. Each line drawn, every character shaped, brings you closer to the mastery of this elegant art form. Calligraphy is a journey of continuous learning and joy in each movement. So as you cap your pen, do so with the satisfaction of time well spent, knowing that with every session, your craft grows stronger.

Cherish the stillness after you've finished, the quiet pride in the marks that you've left behind. They are not just ink on paper, but a testament to your dedication and love for the art. Let this be a tranquil conclusion to your practice, and may the peace it brings stay with you until you write again.

Until next time, let the memory of the flowing ink inspire you, and remember: every word you inscribe is a reflection of your unique voice. Farewell for now, and may your calligraphy journey be as rewarding as the beautiful art you create.